CHALK DRAWINGS

IMAGES BY
LACHLAN J MCDOUGALL

©2023

LACHLAN J MCDOUGALL

LJMCD COMMUNICATIONS

ISBN: 9798367558357

ALL RIGHTS RESERVED. NO PART OF THIS BOOK MAY BE REPRODUCED WITHOUT EXPRESS WRITTEN PERMISSION OF THE AUTHOR.

ALL IMAGES COPYRIGHT LACHLAN J MCDOUGALL

IPSWICH, QUEENSLAND, AUSTRALIA

LACHLAN.MCDOUGALL@GMAIL.COM

LACHLANJMCDOUGALL.WORDPRESS.COM

OR FIND THE ARTIST ON INSTAGRAM (@LACHLANJMCDOUGALL) FACEBOOK (LACHLAN J MCDOUGALL – AUTHOR) AND TWITTER (@AUTHORLACHLAN)

PRINTS OF ALL ARTWORKS IN THIS BOOK ARE AVAILABLE FOR PURCHASE BY VISITING:

ARTPAL.COM/LACHLANMCDOUGALL

OR EMAILING LACHLAN.MCDOUGALL@GMAIL.COM

ONCE AGAIN I'M DRAWN TO THE EPHEMERAL. CHALK DRAWINGS ARE NOT HERE TO LAST, THEY ARE GONE ALMOST AS SOON AS THEY ARE FINISHED AS IS SHOWN IN THE ERASURE IMAGES. THERE IS BEAUTY IN THE REMNANTS, THE LITTLE PIECES LEFT OVER ONCE THE IMAGE IS GONE, THERE IS BEAUTY IN THE FORLORN SLASHES OF A CANVAS IN FLUX.

THE IMAGES THEMSELVES ARE PRIMITIVE EXPLORATIONS COMBINING WITH THE CHILDLIKE WHIM TO ARRANGE CONSTELLATIONS. COMBINED FORCES WITH MY CHILDREN AT TIMES IN AN EXPLORATION OF ART AND PLAY. DIGITAL ALTERATION ALSO PLAYS A PART MANIPULATING THE IMAGE TO CREATE A NEW EPHEMERA FLOATING PRECARIOUSLY OUTSIDE THE CHALKBOARD. THESE ARE IMAGES ON THE EDGE OF THE REAL—THEY ARE A SNAPSHOT IN TIME ALTERED TO A PLACE BEYOND REASON. NO MUSEUM CAN HOUSE THESE WORKS, THEY ARE LOST TO THE WINDS, ONLY THE RECORDINGS REMAIN.

PRIMITIVISM IS OF THE ESSENCE HERE, THE PRIMITIVE CHILD'S HAND THE GLORY OF THE CAVE DRAWING. THE SOLITUDE OF THE LINE THE BRAMBLE OF CHAOS WHEN THESE SIMPLE LINES INTERSECT. THIS IS THE WELLING UP OF IMAGE FROM CHAOS AND DECAY. EACH IMAGE RISES UP FROM THE ASHES OF THE PRECEDING DRAWING AND THE WHOLE THING BLURS TOGETHER IN ONE POT OF VOICES. FROM THE SIMPLE MINIMALIST GRIDWORK TO THE BROAD SWEEP OF THE WHOLE PICTURE, EVERYTHING CHURNS TOGETHER IN ONE ECHOING CACOPHONY.

THESE IMAGES ARE PRODUCED IN A LIMITED RUN ON 10 SIGNED AND NUMBERED PRINTS WITH AN UNSIGNED 'PRINT ON DEMAND' OPTION FOR EASE OF ACCESS AND PROLIFERATION OF ART.

ABSTRACT

16 X 20 INCH

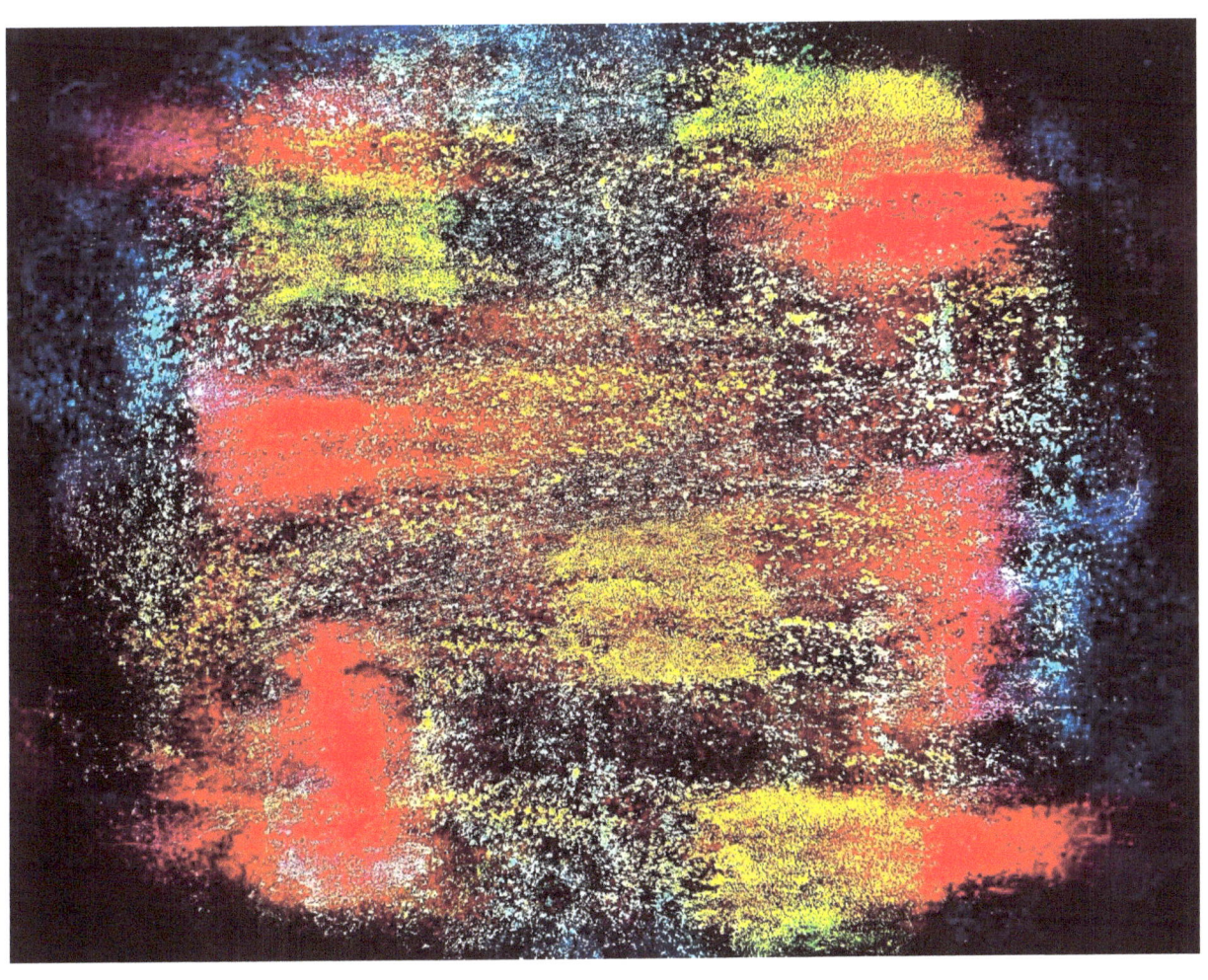

ABSTRACT 2

16 X 20 INCH

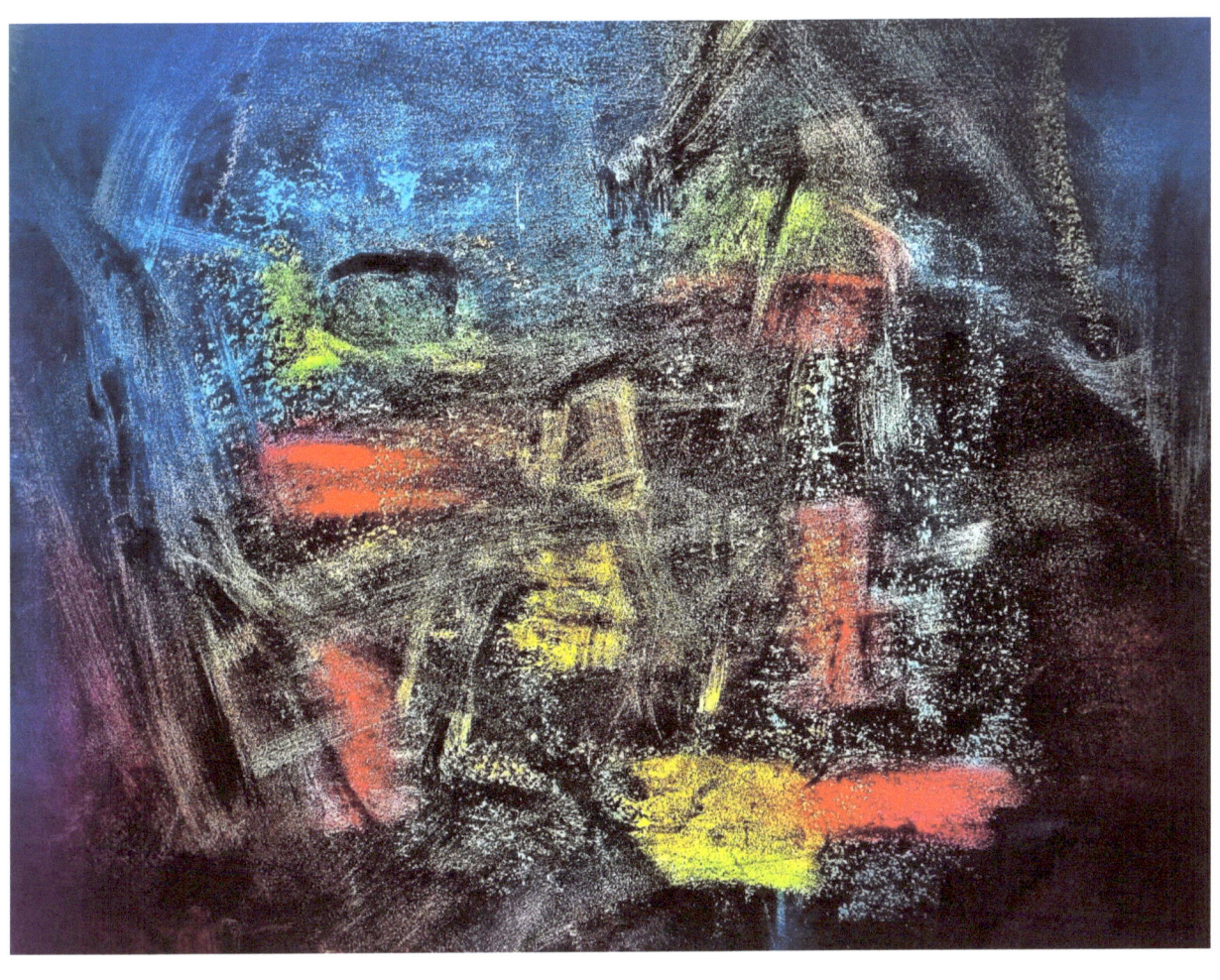

ABSTRACT 3

16 X 20 INCH

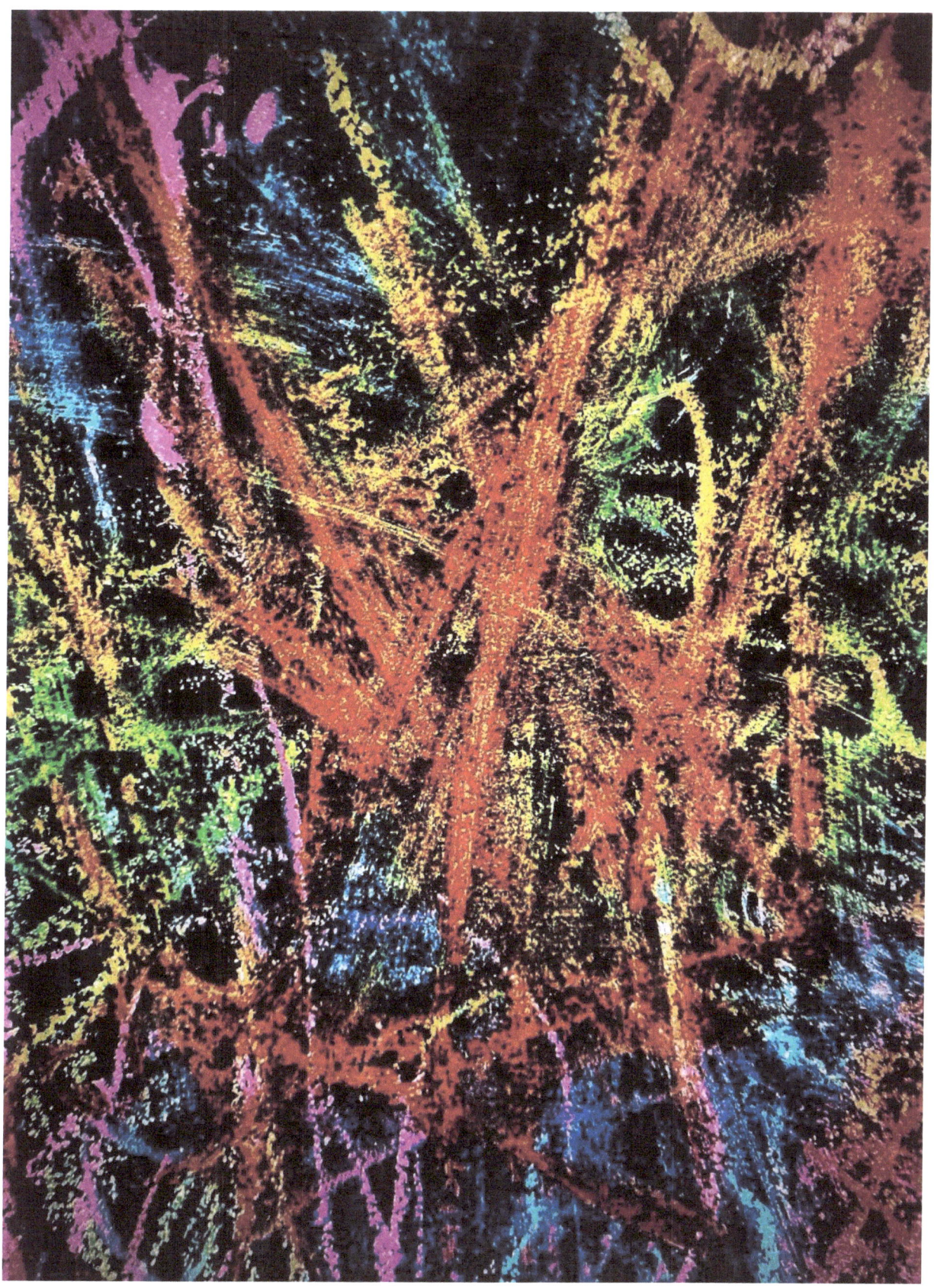

'ARTHUR'

(WITH AC MCDOUGALL)

16 X 20 INCH

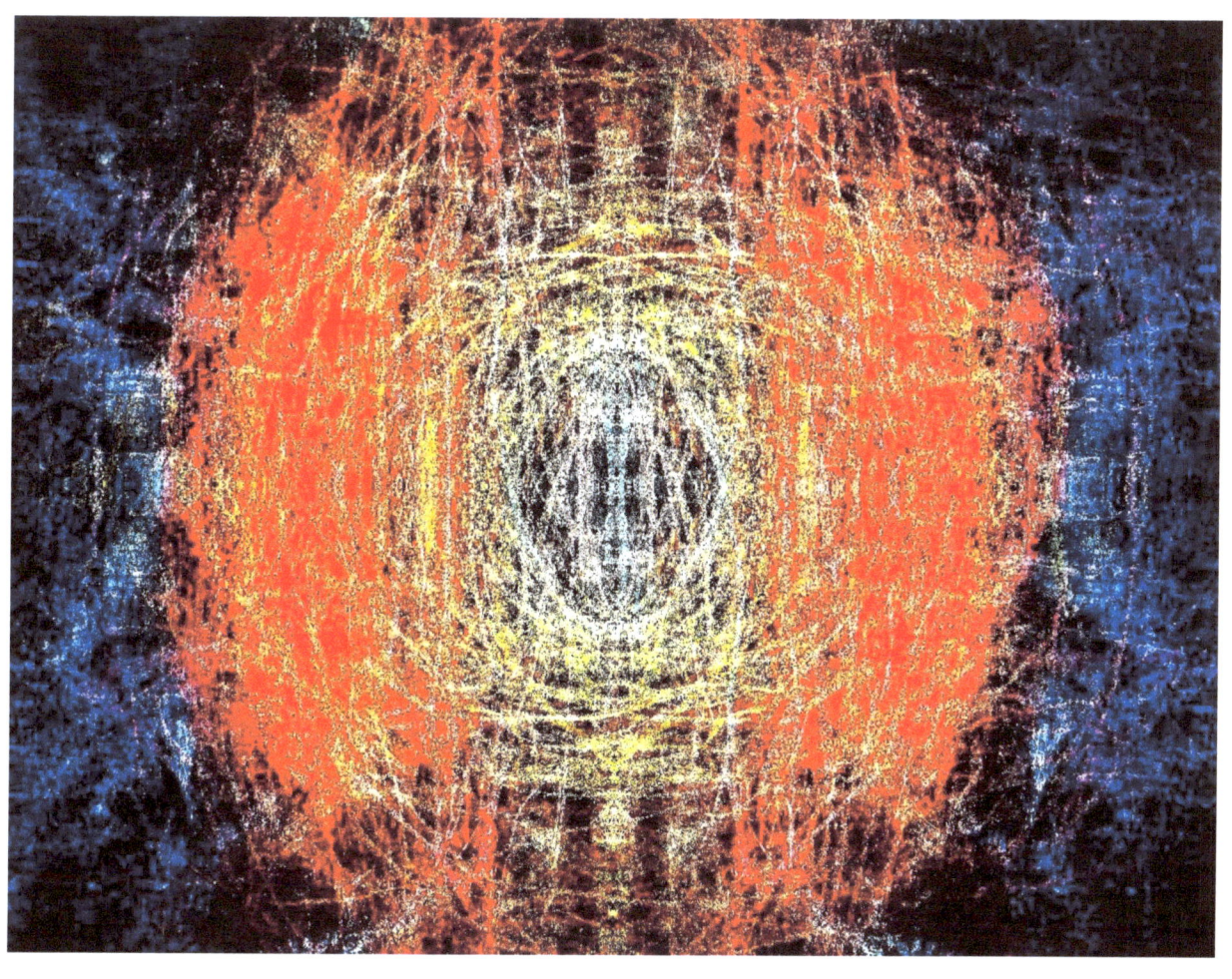

'ARTHUR' 2

(WITH AC MCDOUGALL)

16 X 20 INCH

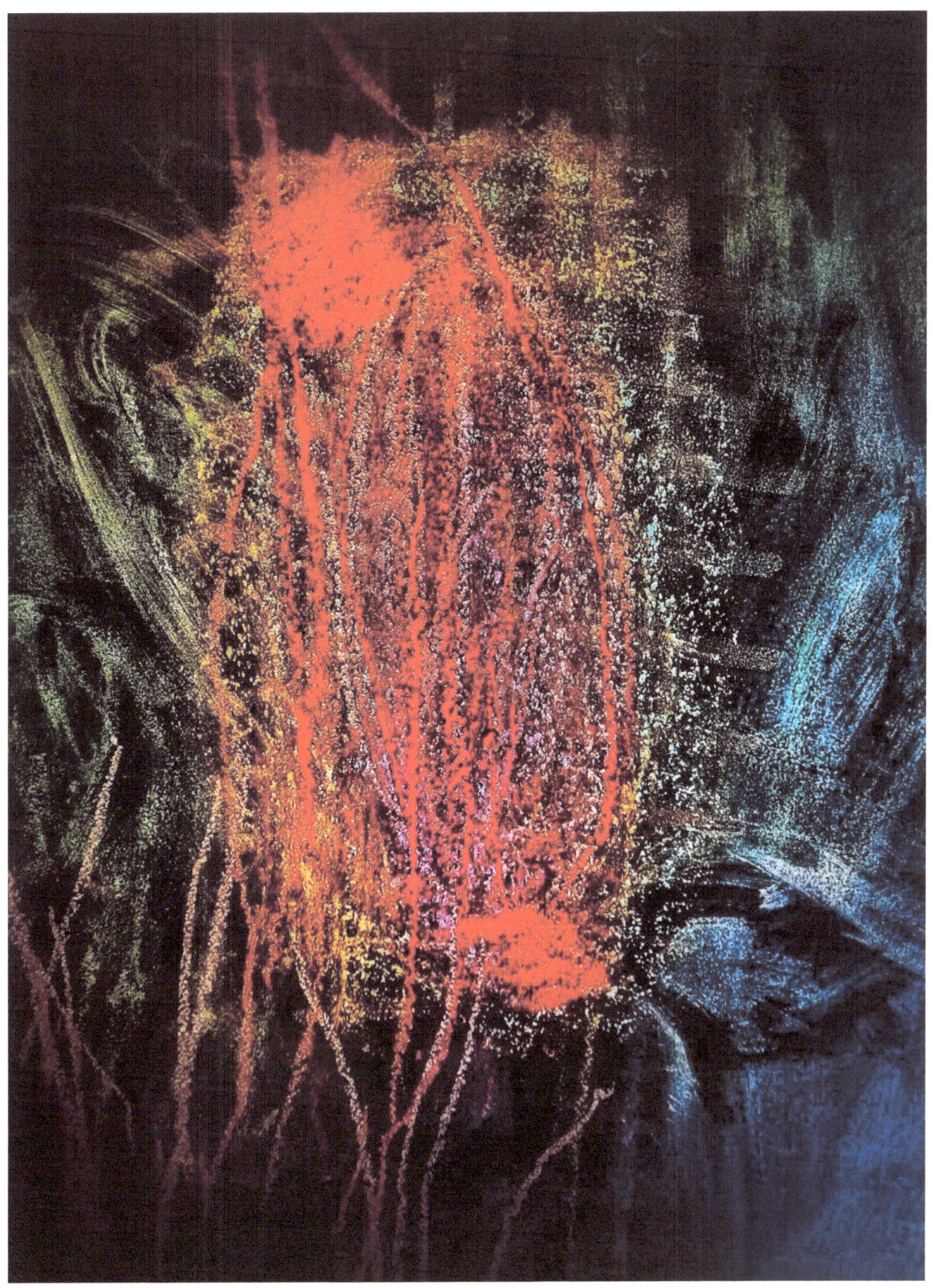

'BLUE'

(WITH AC MCDOUGALL)

16 X 20 INCH

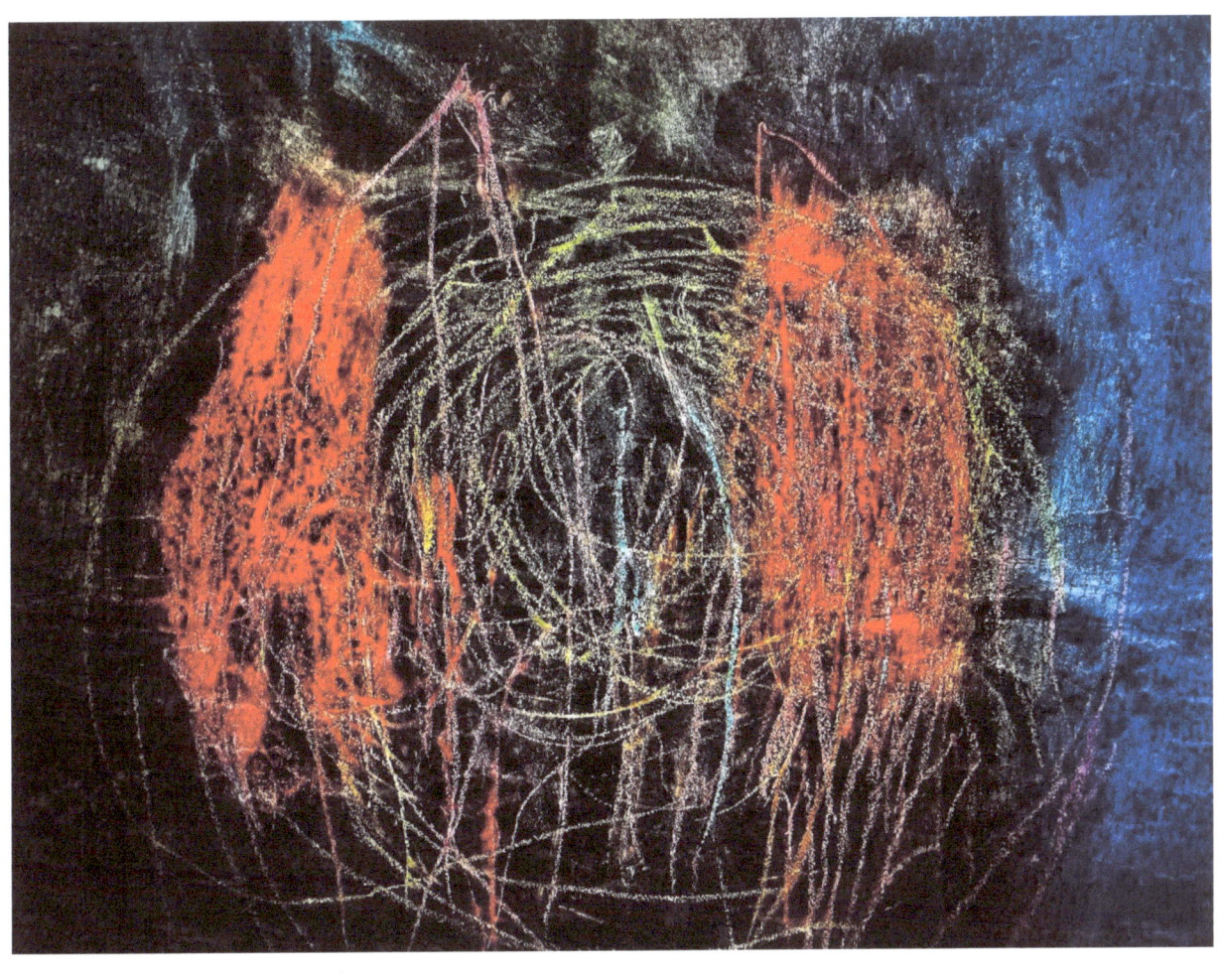

HANDPRINTS IN SUMMER SNOW

(WITH AC AND PB MCDOUGALL)

16 X 20 INCH

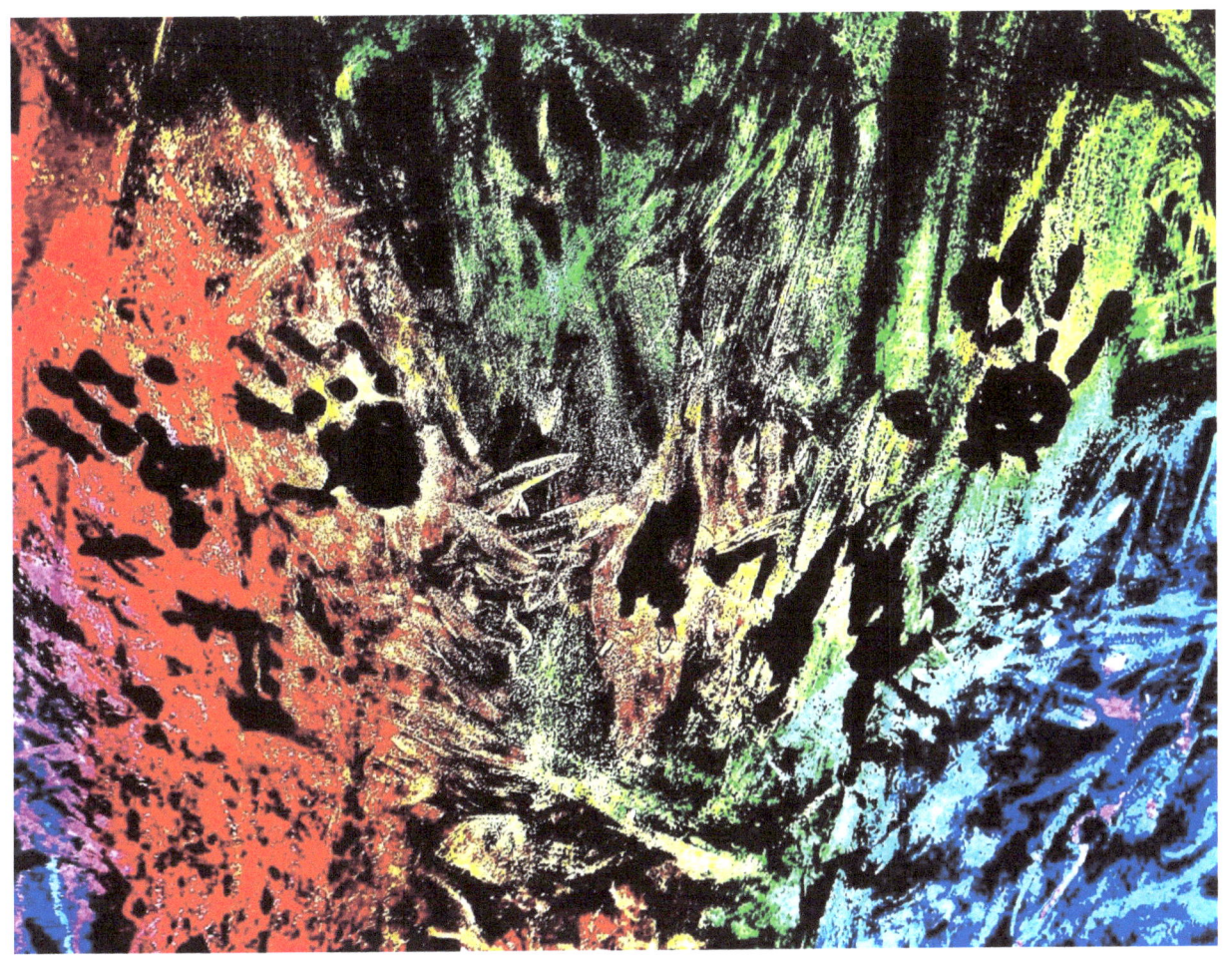

BULB

16 X 20 INCH

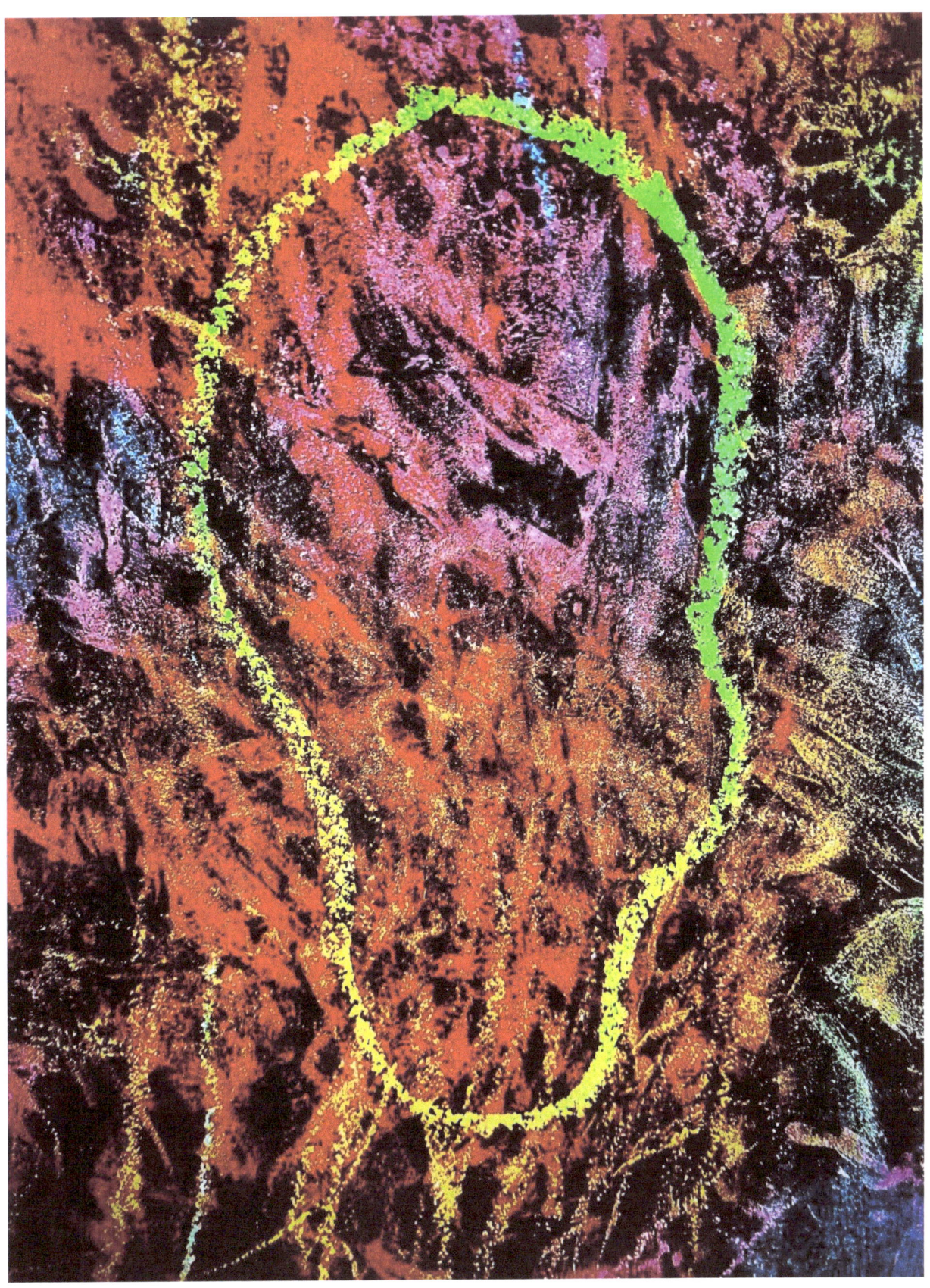

TRICOLOUR

16 X 20 INCH

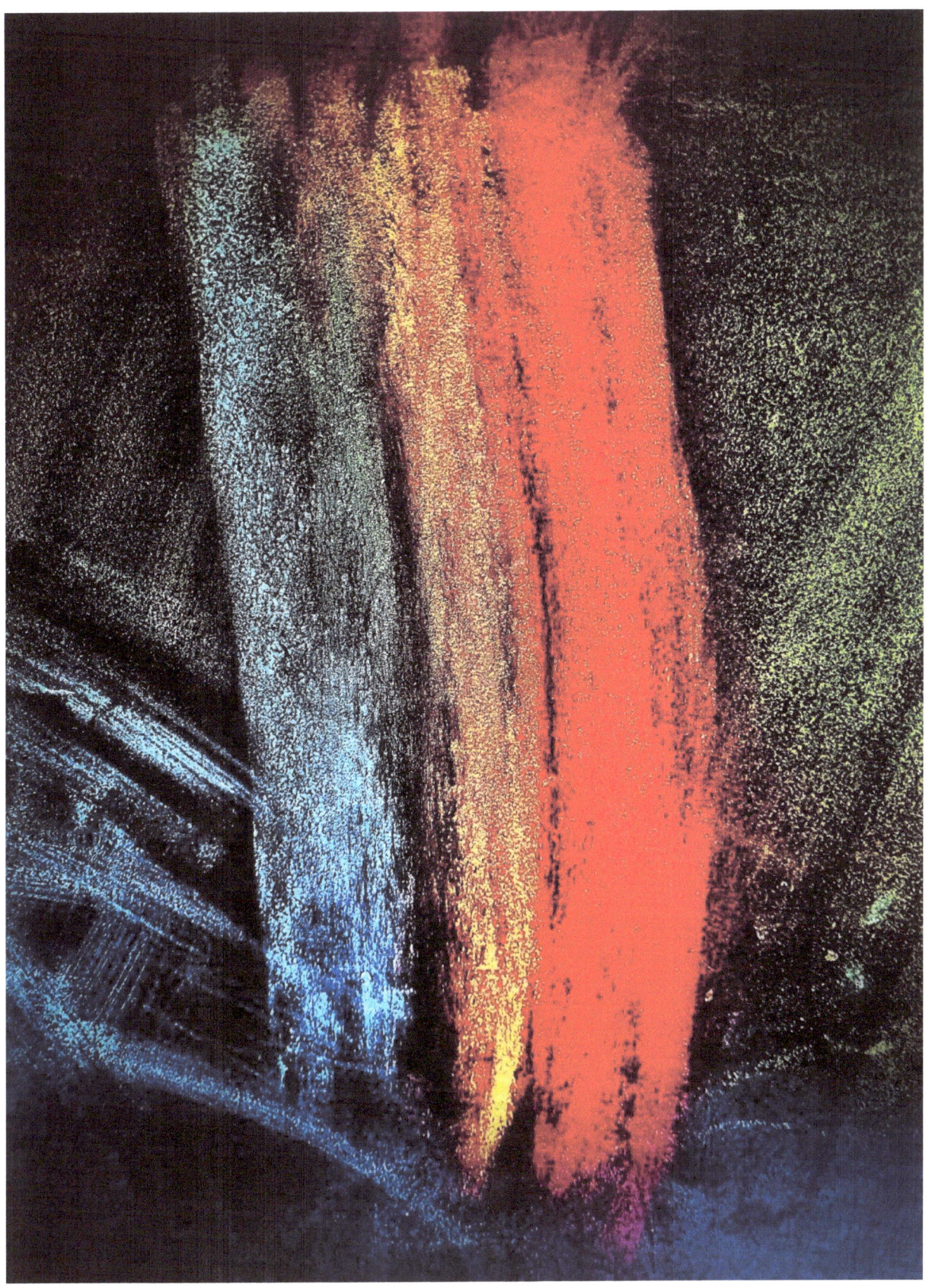

CANDLE

16 X 20 INCH

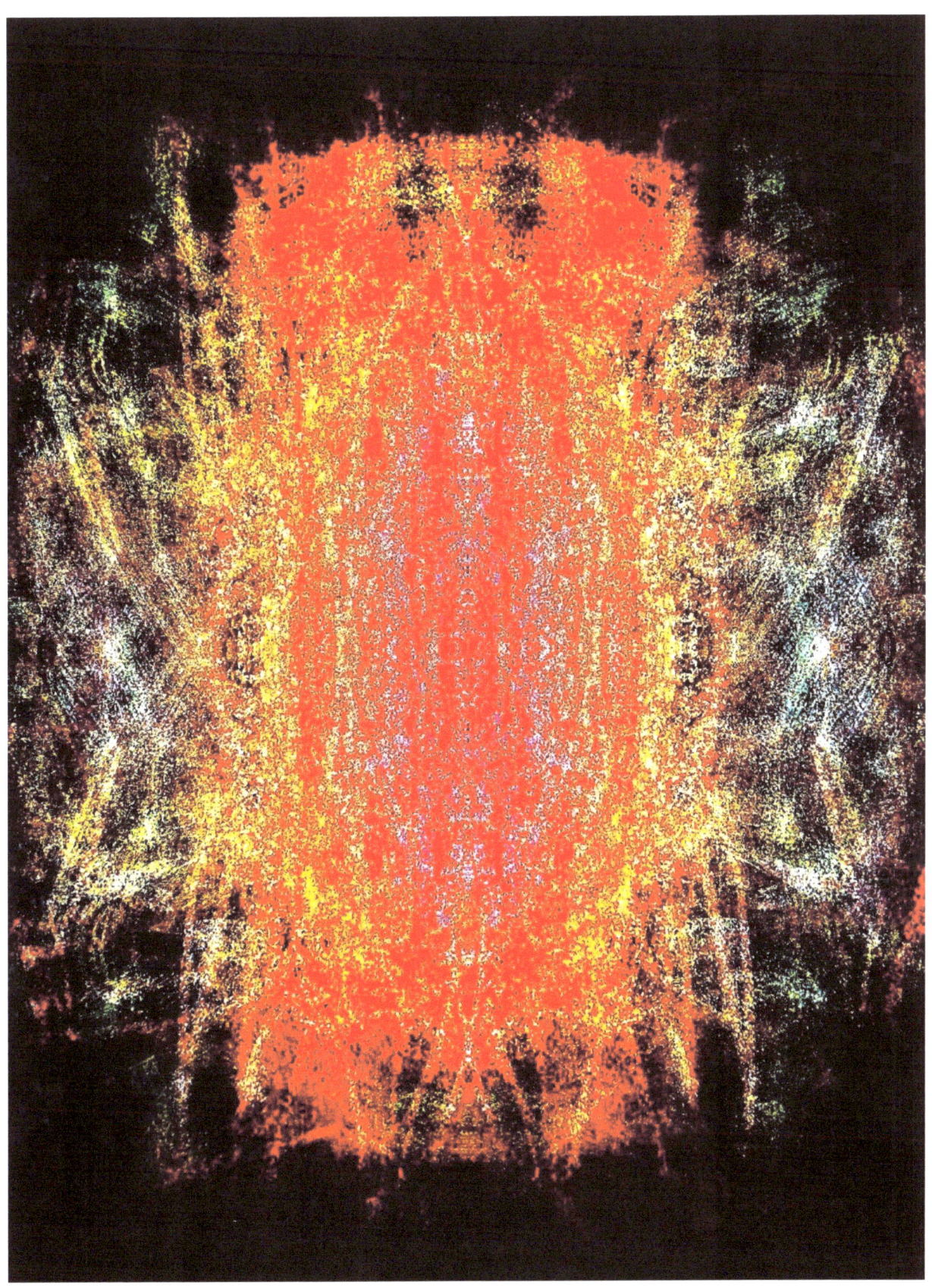

IMPENDING STORM

16 X 20 INCH

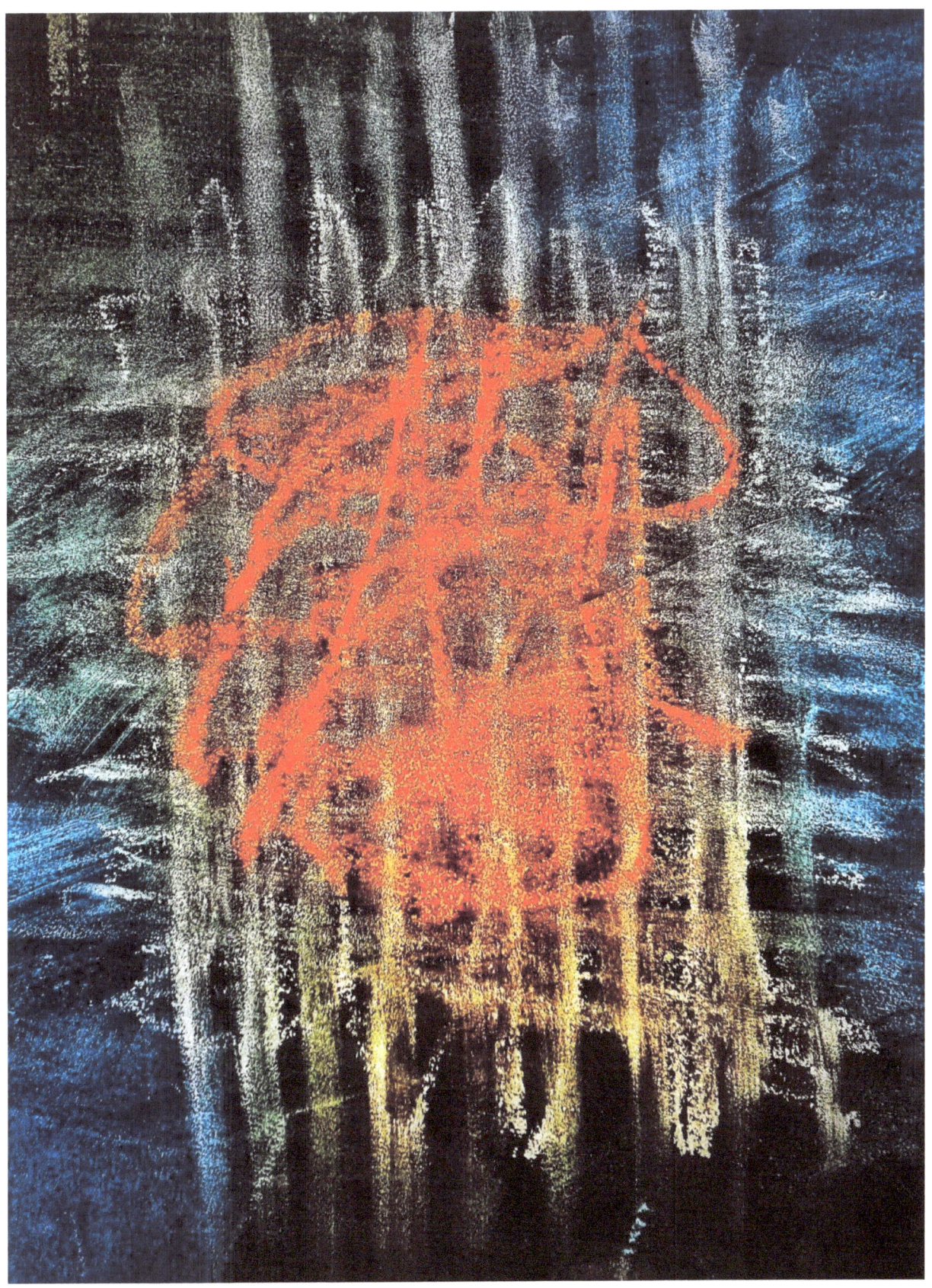

STORM BROKEN

16 X 20 INCH

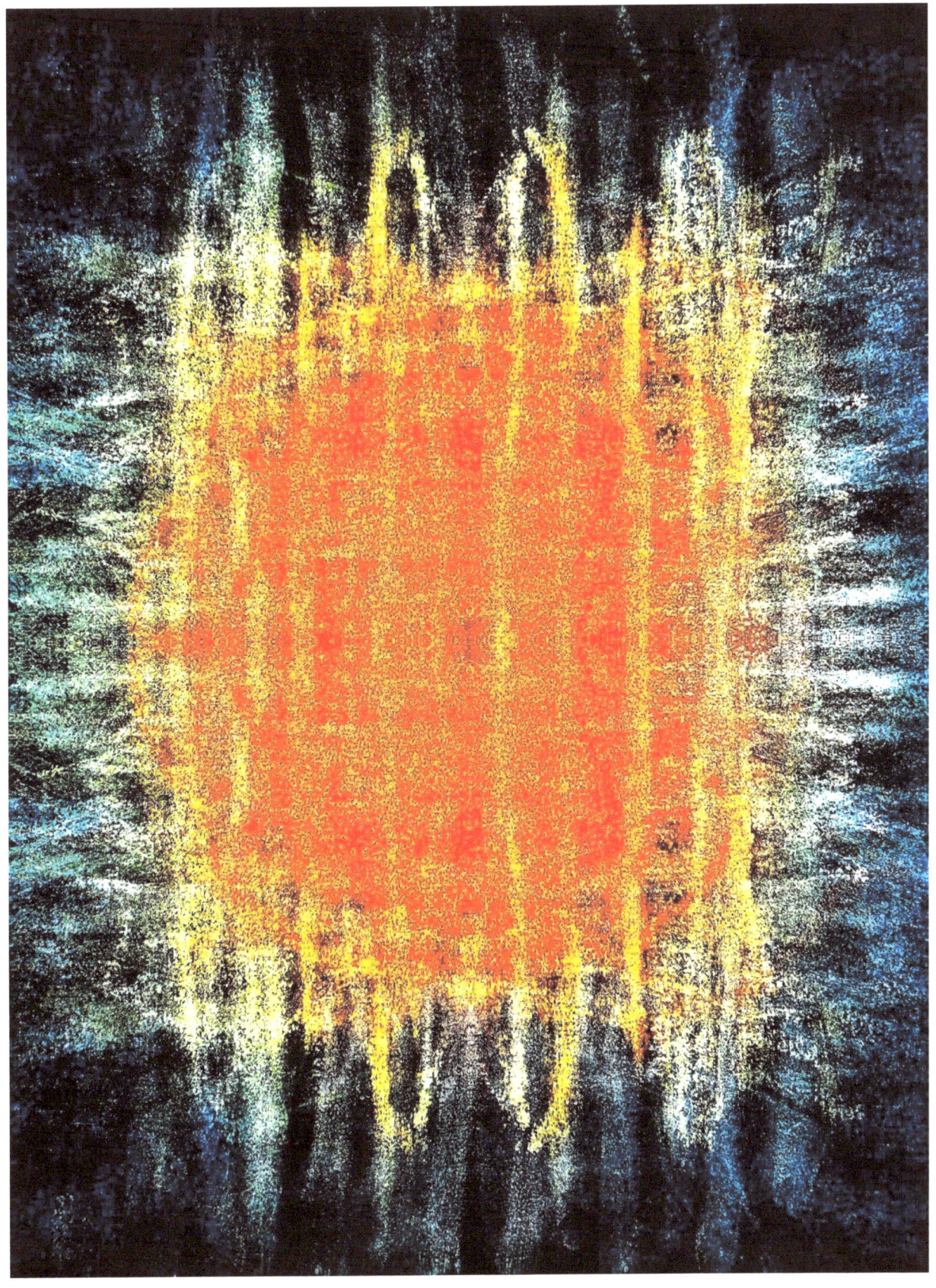

CAVE DRAWING (ARTHUR)

16 X 20 INCH

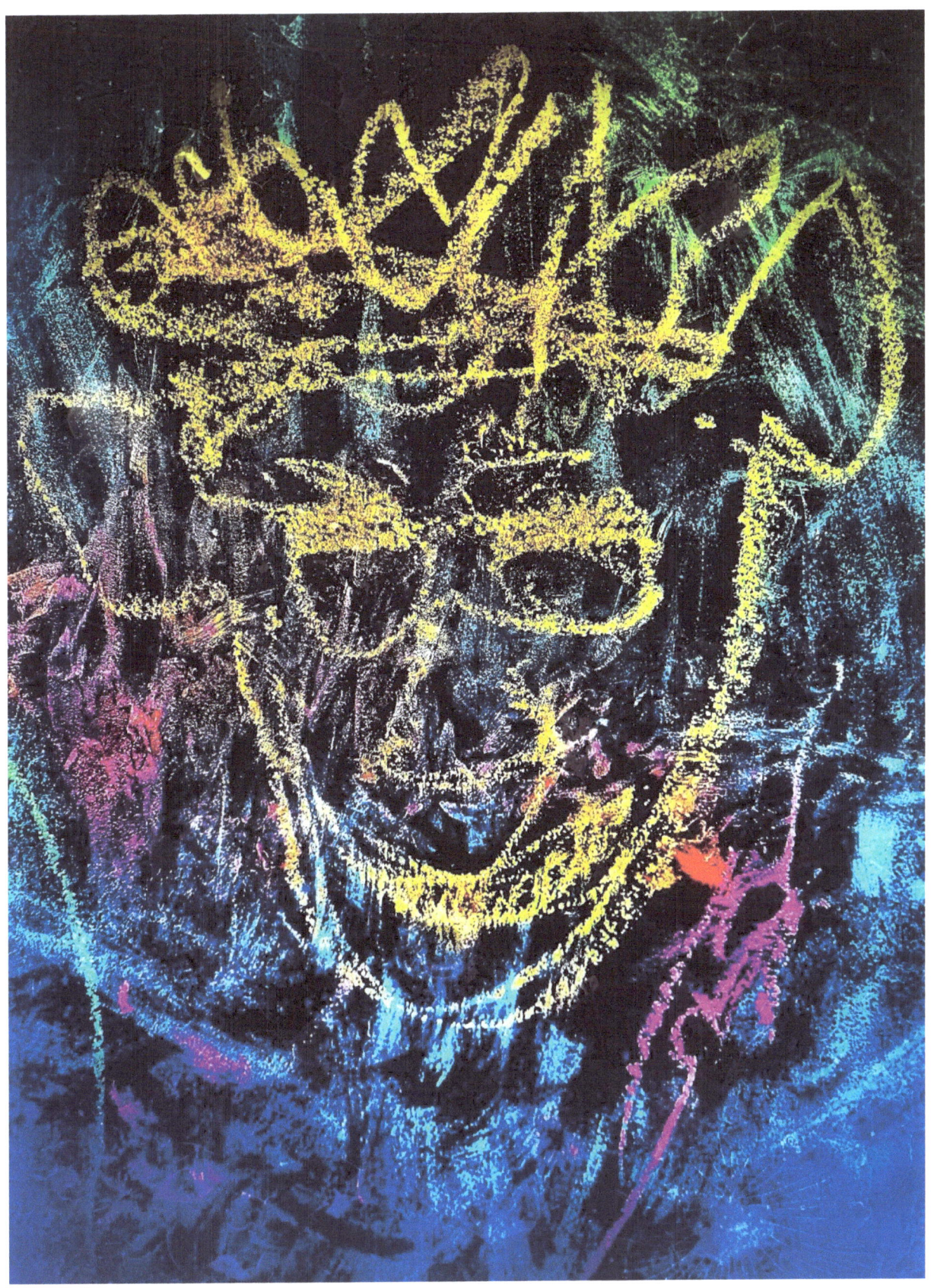

CAVE DRAWING (MONKEY)

16 X 20 INCH

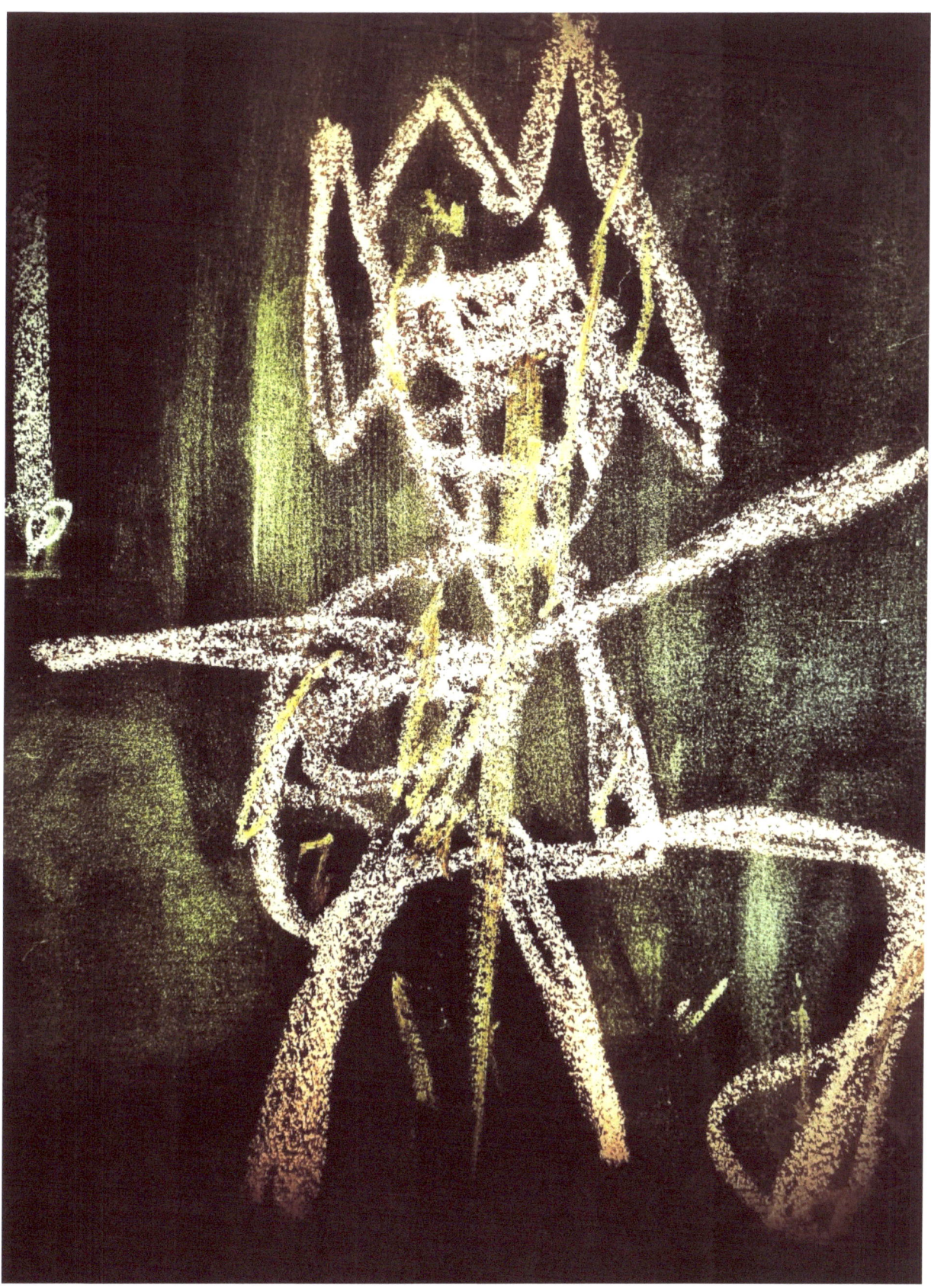

CAVE DRAWING (PATRICK)

16 X 20 INCH

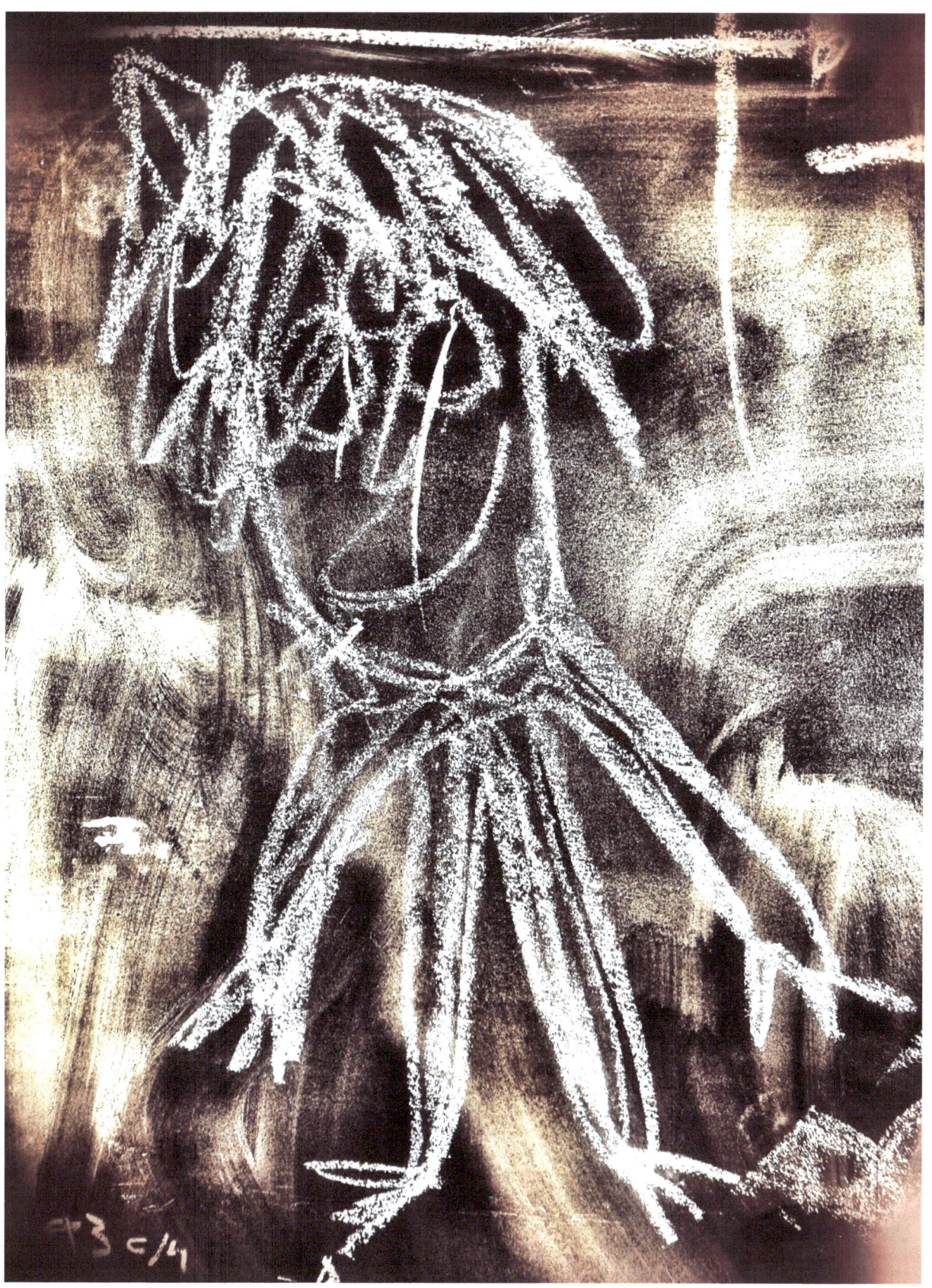

RAINBOW BRIDGE

16 X 20 INCH

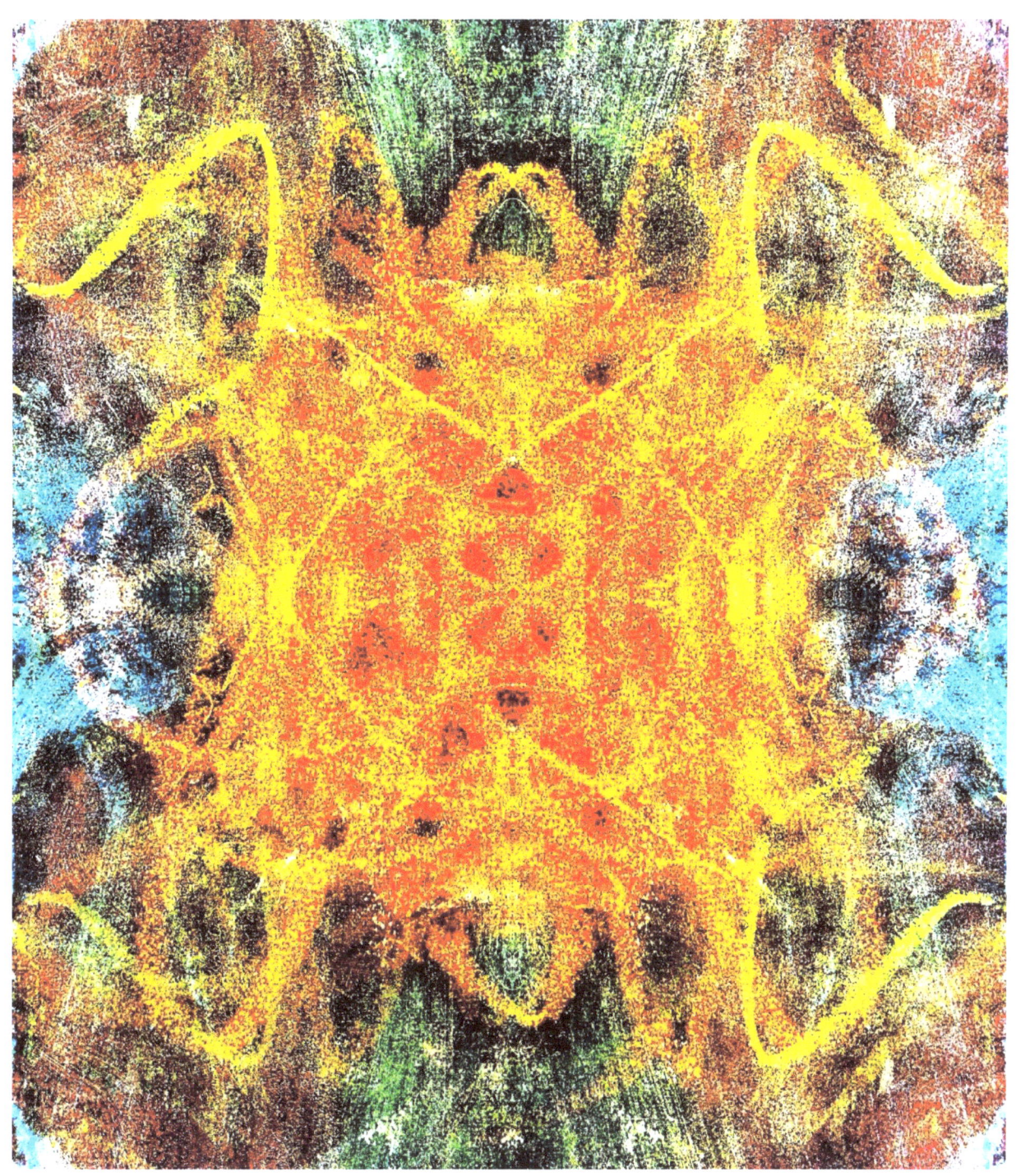

GRID SYSTEM #2

16 X 20 INCH

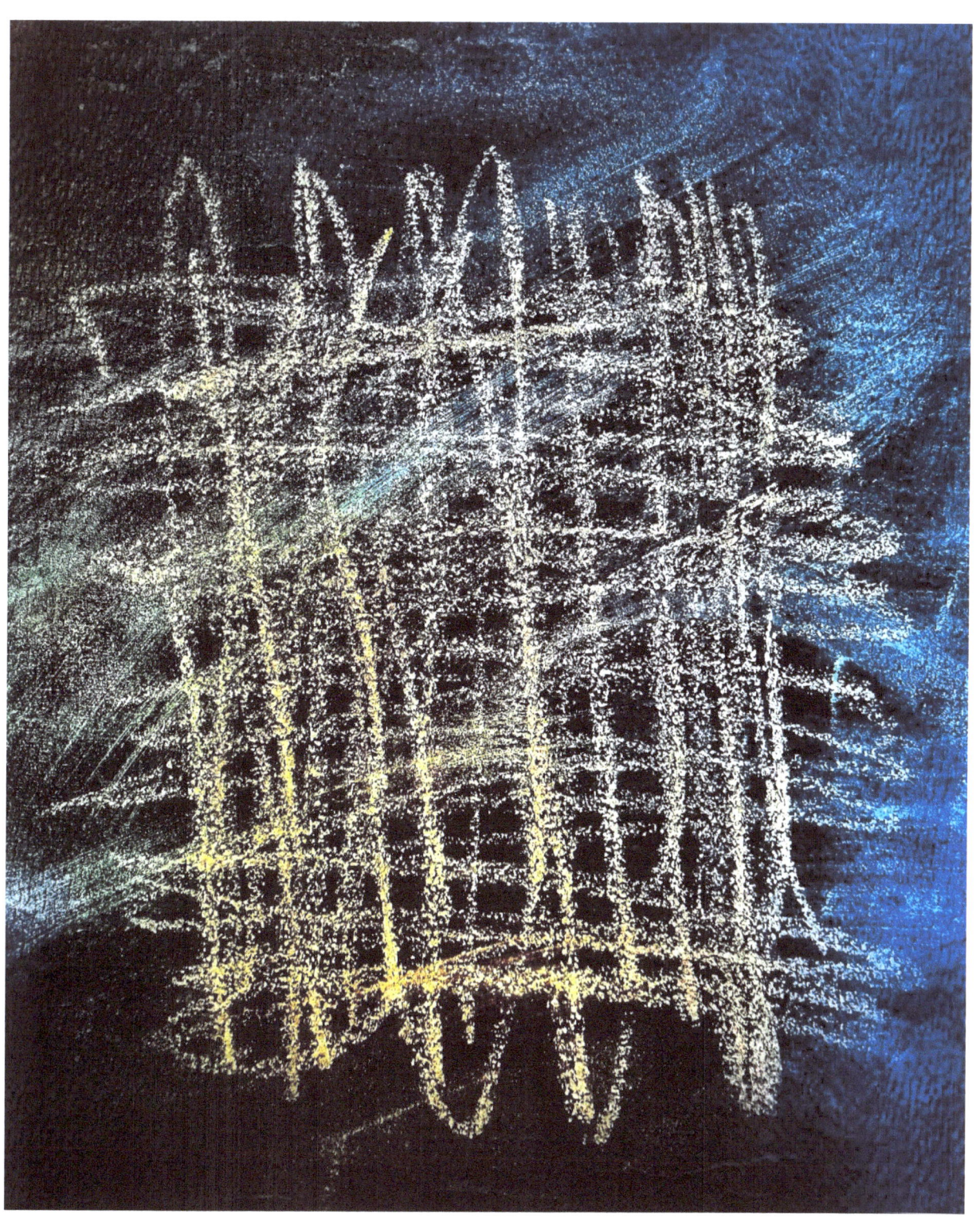

GRID SYSTEM #3

16 X 20 INCH

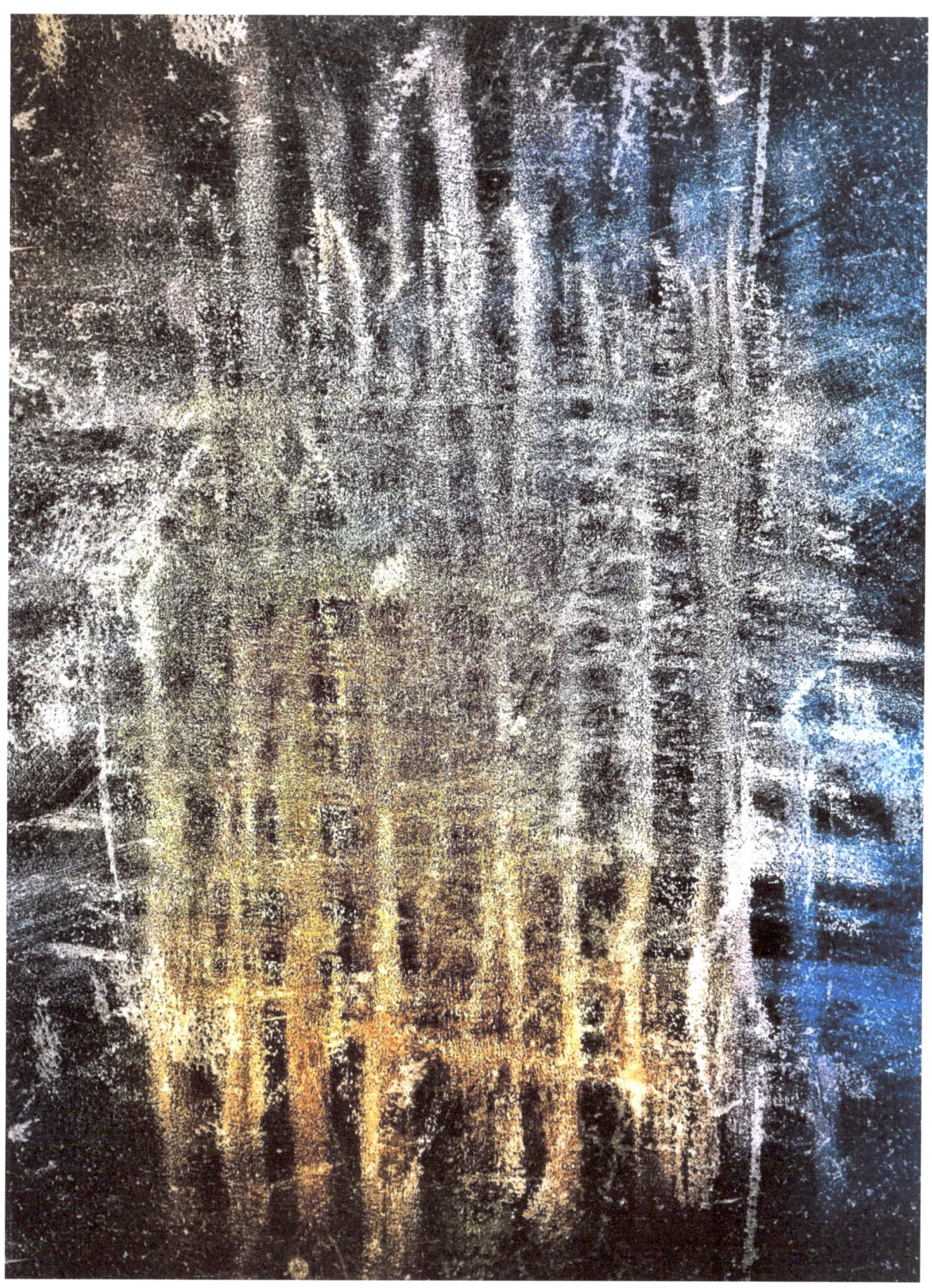

ERASURE 2

16 X 20 INCH

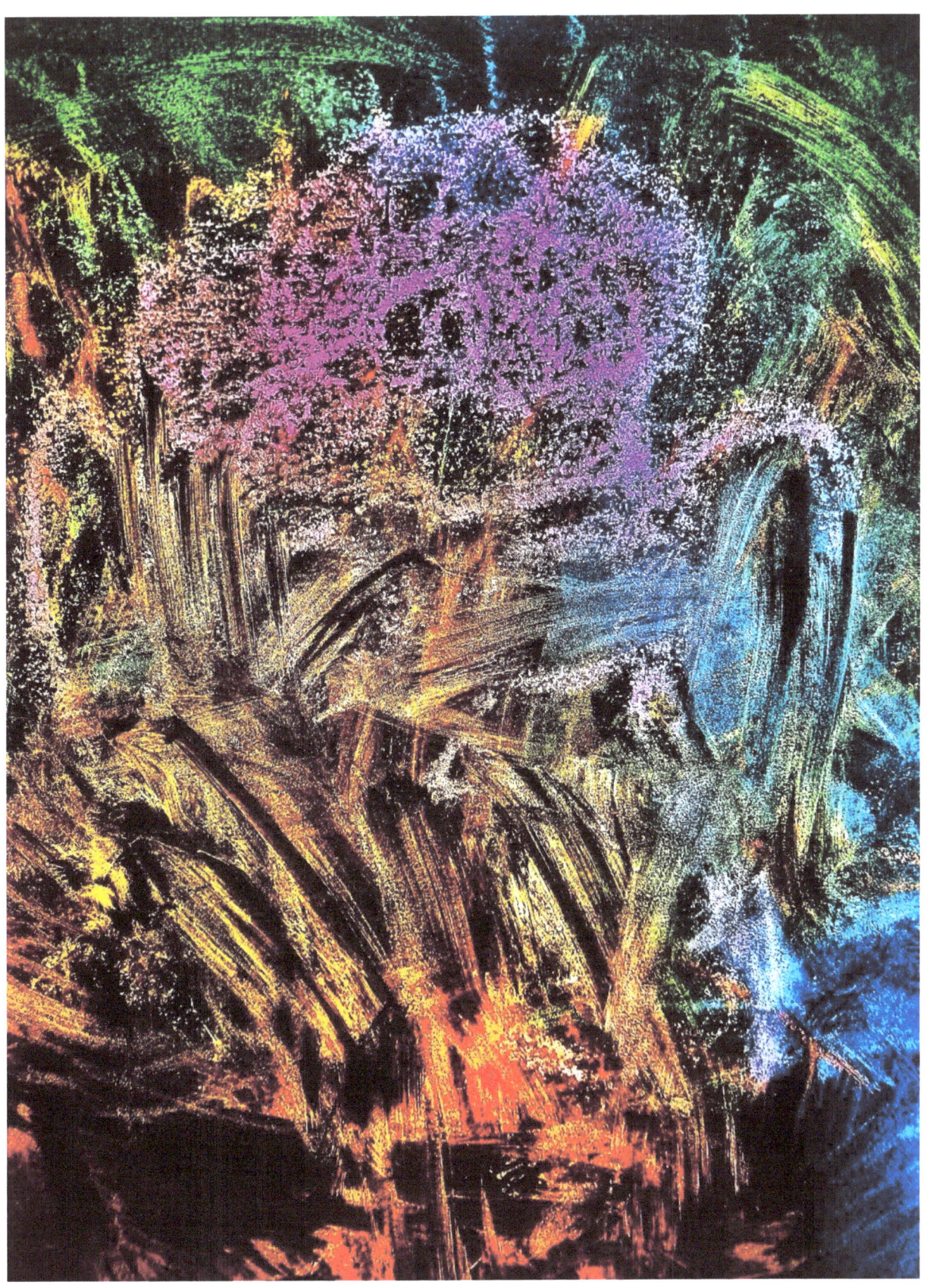

FABLED LEARNING

16 X 20 INCH

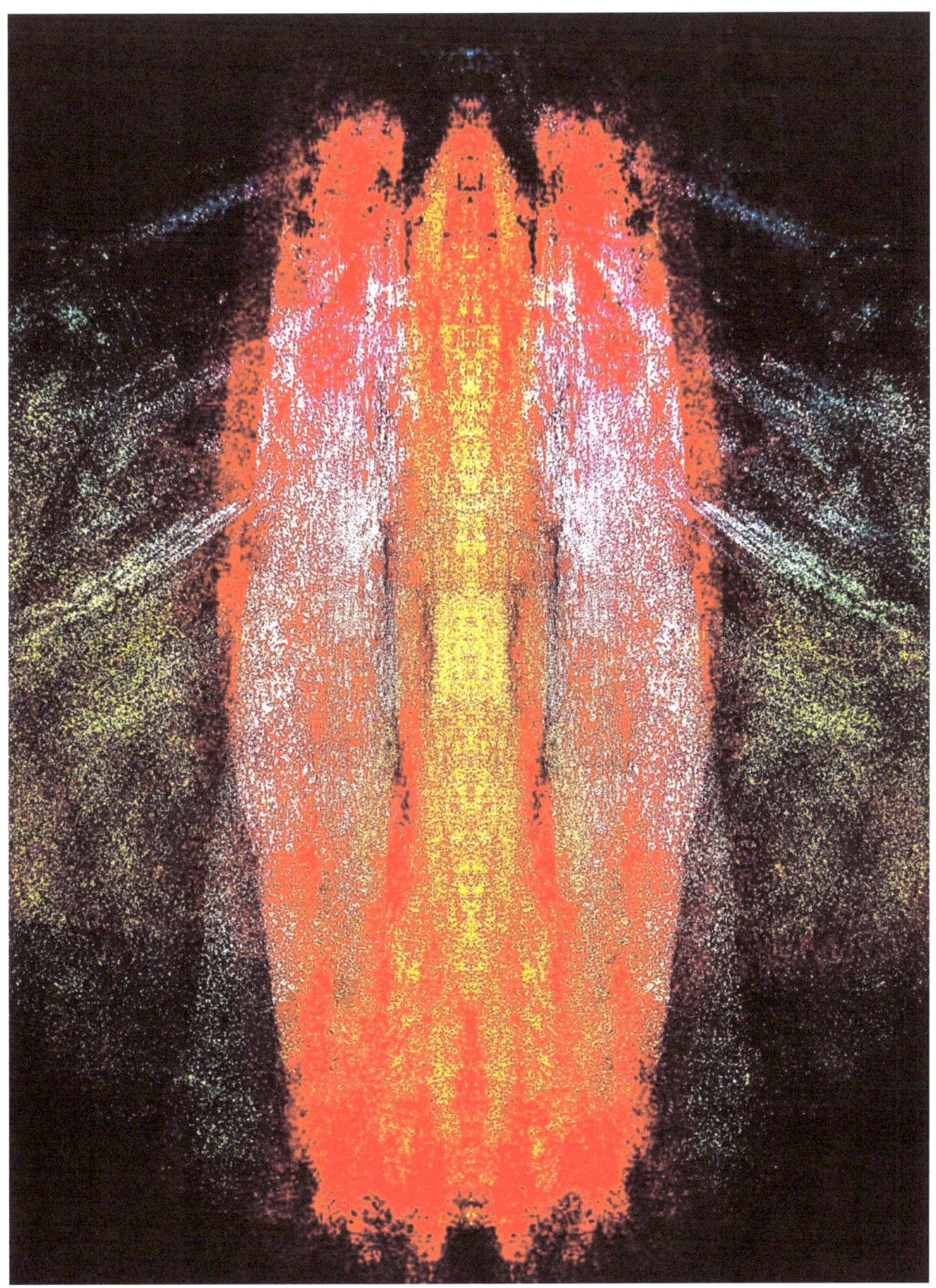

THE WHOLE PICTURE

(WITH AC AND PB MCDOUGALL)

16 X 20 INCH

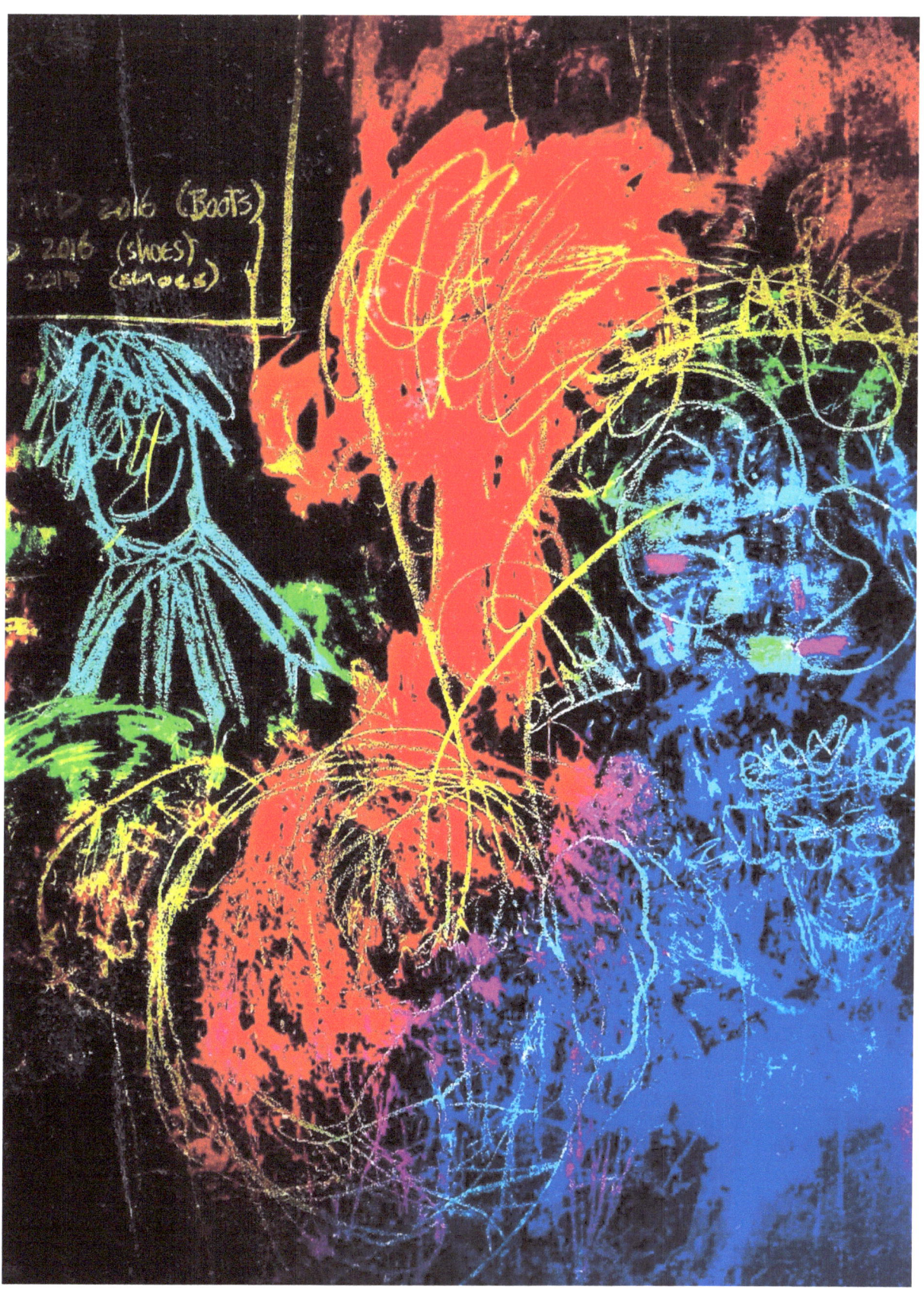

OTHER VISUAL TITLES FROM LACHLAN J MCDOUGALL:

NOTEBOOK SKETCHES

CATALOGUE OF VISUAL ART 2022

TWELVE PHOTOGRAPHS OF SILENCE

NEGATIVELAND

FILE FOLDERS: PAINTINGS IN EPHEMERA

ALL TITLES AVAILABLE FROM AMAZON.COM OR BY EMAILING LACHLAN.MCDOUGALL@GMAIL.COM WITH YOUR ORDER

www.ingramcontent.com/pod-product-compliance
Lightning Source LLC
Chambersburg PA
CBHW051223220526
45473CB00003B/1146